What Others Are Saying

Amazing abundance: the power of imagining, planning, action, patience, and discipline... the power of faith! John has lived these things and has realized amazing abundance. So can you.
—**Dr. Bill Tyler**
Former treasurer and member of the Board of Directors, Seeds of Hope Children's Ministry

Amazing Abundance not only offers practical methods to save and grow your financial wealth, it helps you to rethink and view things more productively. Using examples from his own life, John shows us how prayer and believing in our almighty God brings amazing results to our hard work.
—**Eldon Guenther**
President, 777 Eccounting Systems Inc.

Amazing ABUNDANCE

FOR THOSE WHO STRUGGLE LIVING PAYCHECK TO PAYCHECK

JOHN CHALKIAS

AMAZING ABUNDANCE
Copyright © 2022 by John Chalkias
www.facebook.com/amazinglife4you/
www.johnchalkias.ca

All rights reserved. Neither this publication nor any part of this publication may be reproduced or transmitted in any form or by any means, electronic or mechanical, including photocopying, recording or any information storage and retrieval system, without permission in writing from the author.

All Scripture quotations, unless otherwise indicated, are taken from the Holy Bible, New International Version®, NIV®. Copyright ©1973, 1978, 1984, 2011 by Biblica, Inc.™ Used by permission of Zondervan. All rights reserved worldwide. www.zondervan.com The "NIV" and "New International Version" are trademarks registered in the United States Patent and Trademark Office by Biblica, Inc.™ • Scripture quotations taken from the (NASB®) New American Standard Bible®, Copyright © 1960, 1971, 1977, 1995, 2020 by The Lockman Foundation. Used by permission. All rights reserved. www.lockman.org. • Scripture quotations are from the Revised Standard Version of the Bible, copyright © 1946, 1952, and 1971 National Council of the Churches of Christ in the United States of America. Used by permission. All rights reserved worldwide. • Scripture quotations marked (NLT) are taken from the Holy Bible, New Living Translation, copyright ©1996, 2004, 2015 by Tyndale House Foundation. Used by permission of Tyndale House Publishers, Carol Stream, Illinois 60188. All rights reserved.

Printed in Canada

ISBN: 978-1-4866-2326-6
eBook ISBN: 978-1-4866-2327-3

Word Alive Press
119 De Baets Street Winnipeg, MB R2J 3R9
www.wordalivepress.ca

WORD ALIVE
—P R E S S—

MIX
Paper from
responsible sources
FSC® C103567

Cataloguing in Publication information can be obtained from Library and Archives Canada.

Dedicated to my sons and daughters.
I wish I knew these things when I was your age.

*Beloved, I pray that in all respects you may
prosper and be in good health,
just as your soul prospers.*
(3 John 1:2, NASB)

I came that they may have life, and have it abundantly.
—Jesus (John 10:10, RSV)

a·bun·dance (ə-bŭn′dəns).
Adjective. To have in an ample quantity, plentiful, fullness, or wealth.

Contents

DISCLAIMER	xi
FOREWORD	xiii
CHAPTER ONE: **MONEY IS THE ANSWER TO EVERYTHING**	1
CHAPTER TWO: **YOUR THOUGHTS CONTROL YOUR MONEY**	9
CHAPTER THREE: **WRITE IT DOWN**	13
CHAPTER FOUR: **PRINCIPLE OF INCREASE**	17
CHAPTER FIVE: **POWER OF DOUBLING**	23
CHAPTER SIX: **THE TRAP OF DEBT**	29
CHAPTER SEVEN: **MULTIPLE SOURCES OF INCOME**	35
CHAPTER EIGHT: **MAKING MONEY WHILE YOU SLEEP**	39
CHAPTER NINE: **GOOD DEBT**	45
CHAPTER TEN: **POSSIBILITIES AND PROBABILITIES**	49
CHAPTER ELEVEN: **PERSISTENCE AND VISON**	53
CHAPTER TWELVE: **CHOOSE TO BELIEVE**	57
CHAPTER THIRTEEN: **I ASKED GOD FOR A MILLION DOLLARS**	65
CHAPTER FOURTEEN: **THE BLESSING OF GENEROSITY**	69
CONCLUSION	73
ABOUT THE AUTHOR	77

Disclaimer

I AM NOT a financial planner or advisor, nor would I put myself in the ranks of prosperity preachers. This book is simply my take on poverty and riches after spending more than twenty-five years helping people come out of extreme poverty to a life of hope and victorious living.

If you are drawn by wealth and self-improvement, you might have been drawn by the title. If you are one of those who think money is the root of all evil, you might have picked up this book out of disdain, and maybe a bit of curiosity. In any case, let me encourage you to read on.

King Solomon, in his book of wisdom and in Ecclesiastes, commonly said that he "observed" people. He observed the rich, the poor, the foolish, and the wise and came to conclusions inspired by the Holy Spirit.

The following are simply my observations.

Foreword

YOU MAY WONDER why a missionary who works among the poor would write a book on money, wealth, and generosity. Wouldn't a book on evangelism or compassion be more pertinent?

As important as those issues are, I think John is the perfect person to write this book.

When he asked me to write the foreword, I was immediately intrigued. What would he say? What qualified him to talk about money? But as I read, I realized he is just the voice we need.

Why?

If the biblical principles that speak about money and wealth management don't work in the slums of a Zambian shantytown, we have missed the point of what the Bible teaches. God's principles are transferable to every culture and time, and John comes from a vantage point that demonstrates this truth. Working in the trenches among the poor, he gives us examples which reveal that God's principles for money and wealth work anywhere.

John's goal is not to show you how to become a millionaire or give you three steps to prosperity. Instead he provides us scriptural and practical insight on how to steward the resources God gives us and then leverage them for His glory. John's message echoes the instructions of Paul:

> *Tell them to use their money to do good. They should be rich in good works and generous to those in need, always being ready to share with others. By doing this they will be storing*

up their treasure as a good foundation for the future so that they may experience true life. (1 Timothy 6:18–19, NLT)

The only way we will ever be *"rich in good works and generous to those in need"* is to apply the principles God has given us for making and managing money. This book will help you understand that no matter where you live, who you are, or what you do, it is never too late to begin applying God's principles to your finances.

—**Shawn Vandop**
Lead Pastor, Main Street Church
Chilliwack, British Columbia

Chapter One

MONEY IS THE ANSWER TO EVERYTHING

*A feast is made for laughter, wine makes life
merry, and money is the answer for everything.*
(Ecclesiastes 10:19)

HAVE YOU EVER looked at people walking along a busy street? Did anyone suddenly appear who was so extraordinary that you couldn't stop staring? And as you watched this person, did you get a revelation that changed the way you thought, the way you did ministry, and the way you lived?

Imagine that all this could happen just by observing one person walking by in the crowd.

One day I found myself sitting in a café at Manda Hill, the only mall in Zambia at the time. My wife Susan and I had driven to the capital, Lusaka, from the city of Ndola to purchase supplies for our children's home for HIV-orphaned children.[1] Susan was shopping for children's clothing and small appliances, among other things.

Let me tell you something about me, and by extension about my patient wife. I always feel disoriented and antsy when I'm in a mall. It happens when I'm at home in Canada, too.

That is, unless I'm in a hardware or sporting goods store. Then for some strange reason I'm okay. I can stay in these stores for hours and not have any of those symptoms.

---

[1] Our children's ministry, Seeds of Hope, started as the Buseko Children's Home, the first home for orphaned children affected or infected by HIV/AIDS in Zambia.

I've heard that many other men have the same issue with malls. For me, it seems the only relief comes by letting Susan do the shopping while I find a good coffee shop. Susan feels it's best for me to do this, as she can sense my symptoms coming on as soon as we get near a mall. She says these symptoms are accompanied by lots of whining and complaining, so when I head to the coffee shop it's a win-win.

I was sitting at an outdoor table enjoying a cup of coffee, under the heat of the Zambian sun, while I watched the people going by. Immersed in the sights and sounds of Africa, I saw women in their colorful *chitangies* (dress wraps). Some of them had babies on their backs. Others carried goods on their heads. Rhythmic African music was being piped from the speakers of a nearby store. Street vendors tried to sell their goods in the parking lot as people parked their cars. A swirling sea of color, sounds, and smells surrounded me.

Then I noticed something astonishing: an African man in a business suit was walking hand in hand with his young daughter. Her hair was beautifully braided and she was dressed in a frilly white dress and black patent shoes. Licking an ice cream cone and holding her daddy's hand, she couldn't have been more content! It reminded me of when my girls were little and I would take them to Dairy Queen. I loved the laughter and adoration they had for me when I, their dad, took them out and spent time with them.

I continued looking at this father and daughter as they passed. Maybe I was even staring. In my mind, I wondered if he was a diplomat working in one of the embassies, or perhaps an executive in one of the large companies headquartered in Lusaka.

You might wonder why I was so intrigued by this pair. If I had been in North America, I wouldn't have looked twice. But this was the first time I had seen such a sight in Zambia. Culturally, Zambian men do not show affection in public. You won't see them holding their wives' hand while walking down the street. You won't see them showing affection to their children either.

Well, at least I hadn't seen it where we worked in the slums of Ndola. I had seen quite the opposite: neglect, abuse, drunkenness, and abandonment. I'd seen women bear the brunt of raising children while also being the breadwinners. Most of the men I'd seen there had been broken by extreme poverty and hopelessness.

So this was quite the refreshing scene.

About an hour later, Susan came and found me. She parked the full shopping cart next to the table and sat down.

"You know," I said, still thinking about the man and his daughter, "economics is what makes the difference!"

"What?" She looked at me, confused. "What are you talking about?"

I explained what I had observed, and apparently it was something she already knew. Of course economics makes all the difference!

Well, to me it had been like a lightbulb turning on. This was the beginning of my quest to find the balance between giving someone a hand up and not creating dependence in them, as in the case of the proverbial man being taught to fish.

A missionary who worked for an organization that taught modern agriculture and efficiencies once told me that he could tell the level of despair in a village by their garbage and what they planted.

I didn't know what he was talking about.

He went on to explain that when he goes to new a village, he observes their garbage. If the whole village looks like a dump, he knows they're living with a high level of despair and hopelessness.

"John, have you ever been in the house of someone who was depressed?" my friend asked. "You'll notice that they don't clean up. Their house is a mess. People without hopes and dreams don't clean up."

Immediately I pictured in my mind the slums where the kids in our orphanage came from. Those shantytowns were littered with garbage—household garbage, old packages, plastic bags, food wrappers, water bottles, empty beer bottles, etc. People just discarded whatever they used, anywhere and everywhere.

"What about the plants, though?" I asked. "What do plants have to do with anything?"

"When we start a project in a village, we'll find people growing maize, vegetables, and potatoes to eat," he said. "But you won't see any flowers. When we leave, it's heartwarming to see homes with beautiful flower planters. People without hope don't grow flowers. They'll grow food, but not flowers. Flowers are grown by people who have dreams and hopes."

So raising a person's economic level is about more than just money. It's about giving them the ability to dream and the dignity to create or earn income on their own.

The following chart illustrates how having wealth, or not having it, in the third world affects people. To a very large extent, this applies in the western world too!

A middle-class person living in a modern developed country	A poor person living in the developing world
Has wealth or access to wealth.	Is poor or has very limited access to money.
Is educated, has access to education, or is literate.	Is uneducated, has limited access to education, or is illiterate.
Lives in a safe house with running water, electricity, warmth, and a roof that doesn't leak.	Lives in a house that is not safe, with no running water or amenities; the roof leaks or the house is cold.
Has good comfortable furniture.	Has very few furnishings.
Has access to good nutrition.	Has very poor nutrition.
Has modern appliances and conveniences.	Has old and sometimes primitive cooking methods; there is no refrigeration.
Lives in a safe neighborhood.	Lives in an unsafe neighborhood.
Has safe, clean drinking water.	Contends with contaminated water and waterborne and parasitical diseases.

Has access to modern medicine, drugs, and care.	Has limited and poor medical care.
Is confident of opportunities for their children.	Is worried for their children's future; there is a high mortality rate.
Is confident to change their job or career.	Is afraid to lose their job.
Has investments, bank accounts, credit, insurance, etc.	Has no credit or access to extra finances; can only access very high interest rates or is enslaved by moneylenders.
Has a retirement fund.	Has no retirement fund.
Questions authority and has a voice.	Does not question authority and has no voice.
Can confront authority and is aware of their rights.	Runs from authority and has no rights.
Is confident in the legal system.	Distrusts the legal system.
Is confident to suggest their own thoughts and ideas.	Will not suggest their own thoughts and ideas.
Has access to travel/family vacations/recreation.	Has no access to travel/family vacations/recreation.
Expects a long lifespan.	Has a short lifespan.
Sets goals and feels like they can get ahead if they work hard; is able to measure success and feel like they have the power to change their lives for the better.	Feels powerless to change their lot in life; feels hopeless and accepts defeat.
Feels entitled.	Feels exploited.

You will notice that those on the right have limitations on everything from wealth to education, housing, medical care, and safety.

Some people in the impoverished column are able to fight their way out by sheer determination. Think of immigrants who escape severe poverty, wartorn countries, persecution, and hardships through incredible sacrifice and determination. They come to North America with nothing more than a suitcase and their dreams, and many of them become business owners, entrepreneurs, and professionals.

Others are driven back by failure, disease, or injustice. Still others, the majority, are too discouraged to even try.

So the first thing to do is to remove the limitations, whether they are real or imagined.

How can you change?

I will make a strong statement you may need to re-read: you are where you are because you choose to be there. If you didn't choose to be there, you wouldn't remain there.

A lot of people will be upset and offended by this statement.

The reason that some people escape poverty is that they put their mind to it. As difficult as it was, failure was not an option. They made a decision to better their lives and those of their family members.

The good news is that your mind has wings. It will allow you to go to places and do things you can only imagine. It also has anchors that could, if you allow them, keep you where you are for the rest of your life and convince you that there's nothing else for you.

For those of you not living in a developing country, how do economics make a difference in your life? Which column in that chart reflects your thinking and reality?

This is an important question to think about because your economic situation makes all the difference in the world. It determines where you live, where you go to school, the type of medical care you get, the food you eat, and the bed you sleep in. It also determines the sports your kids play, the clubs they join, and even whether they are able to get braces.

Everything depends on your financial situation. It's worth adding that finances are among the biggest issues that lead to marital conflict, and even divorce.

There are many ways to become wealthy. You can spend your life working so much that you fail to enjoy life. All you do is work. You can rob or cheat people. You can be so obsessed with money that you fail to enjoy the beauty of life, and in the process drive everyone away by your stinginess. You can be a tyrant, ruthlessly using people to your own advantage.

But that's not the path to wealth that God has in mind for you. He has a better way and he adds no trouble to it (Proverbs 10:22). Isn't that an amazing thought? That is real abundance.

First let's define what real abundance is.

Real wealth is first knowing Christ as your savior. Everything we do, everything we are, has eternal value. The Bible puts it this way: *"what does it profit a man to gain the whole world, and forfeit his soul?"* (Mark 8:36, NASB)

Secondly, I would say that if you want to know real wealth, you should make the Bible your financial playbook. In it you will find not only the secrets to riches but also the key to experiencing meaningful life and relationships, health in your body, and peace of mind even in the most troublesome times.

If this interests you, then read on. I have more to share with you.

Chapter Two

YOUR THOUGHTS CONTROL YOUR MONEY

*For the love of money is a root
of all kinds of evil.
(1 Timothy 6:10)*

FOR HUNDREDS OF years, and still to this day, many believers and churches have believed and taught that wealth is worldly, unspiritual, unholy, greedy, prideful, and immoral. You may not hear it outright from the pulpit anymore, but certainly you'll notice pious poverty lingering in the undertone of many sermons and church body conversations.

I'll give you an example. Some years ago, a woman came to visit my wife in our home. As they were having coffee, this woman looked at our oak coffee table and commented, "Isn't this table a little pricy for missionaries?"

Later Susan told me about the incident with tears in her eyes. "Can I not have something nice without being judged?"

This woman somehow thought that, being missionaries, we had taken a vow of poverty. Had this woman asked, she would have found out that Susan had bought that particular piece of furniture secondhand, but the principle remains. Even if she'd bought it new at full price, why would we not be allowed to have nice things?

This is an example of pious poverty.

People who are brought up with this type of teaching make a judgment that rich people are greedy. This even shows up in our idle conversations: "So-and-so is rich because he's corrupt" or "That man is *filthy* rich" or "The rich keep getting richer." This kind of thinking affects our subconscious and tells us that being wealthy is bad.

We hear it in the political arena as politicians try to win over voters. They say things like "I'll tax the upper class!" as though the members of the upper class are villains. We see it in children's stories, too, such as Robin Hood stealing from the rich and giving to the poor. We justify this in our minds because we associate wealth with greed. We judge it as evil.

Most people never say out loud that it's bad to be wealthy, but subconsciously that's what they believe.

So where does the trouble come in? More than ninety-five percent of our behavior is driven by the subconscious mind. This means that you need to examine where you've erected limitations for yourself. You can never achieve that dream house or that salary or the wealth you dream of if deep down you think it's a bad thing. Why would you ever achieve something that you think is evil or that you judge other people for?

Other times, subconsciously, you might think you don't deserve to have a better life, bigger bank account, and financial freedom. You might tell yourself you aren't smart enough, educated enough, or good enough because of the bad things you've done or the bad things that have happened to you.

This is called cognitive bias, where your subconscious mind sabotages your dreams and hopes. Most of the time, these thoughts aren't even your own, but rather things people have told you from a young age. A parent or teacher may have planted these seeds of limitations, causing you to believe lies about yourself: "You're not smart enough. You'll never amount to anything." These thoughts are recorded in your mind and become the wall you hit every time you try to get ahead. Often you won't even try, because you believe the lies you've been told.

These reactions are automatic and most people aren't even aware why they do what they do. Your cognitive biases latch on to out-of-context scriptures fragments such as "Money is the root of all kinds of evil" instead of the actual scripture, which tells us that *"the love of money is the root of all kinds of evil"* (1 Timothy 6:10). Your cognitive bias may embrace that one fragment and completely disregard the multitude of scriptures that talk about God's blessing and abundance.

I want to be very clear here: I'm not saying that all believers should be wealthy. That isn't true. What I'm saying is that we often miss out on God's incredible blessings because we live with a poverty mindset.

For the people I work with in Africa, their history is one of being colonized and exploited for centuries. They have grown up in slums. Their parents and grandparents have grown up in shantytowns, townships, and villages. Poverty and exploitation have been the norm and it's reflected in their work habits, conversations, and attitudes about money. Understandably, wealth isn't possible in that poverty mindset.

These people are rich in beauty and joy and goodness and friendship and great humanity. They have the same love for their children that more privileged parents do. What prevents them from moving out of poverty is systemic and generational.

But it is changeable.

I've met people in the lower castes in India, or the stateless hilltribe people in Thailand. What do you think their attitude and thoughts are towards wealth and the ability to get it? Their subconscious thoughts revolve around day-to-day survival, not abundance.

We all have a subconscious belief system that dictates our behavior. This is called our paradigm. Some of us operate with rosy glasses on, and others have a very dim view of the world. We find ourselves in a variety of situations. Some are born into affluence. Others are born into poverty. Still others are born in the continuum between the two.

But your starting point in life doesn't have to define where you end up. You don't need to settle. You don't need to accept your present circumstance as God's will. No matter your current circumstance, you can make practical moves to improve your lifestyle and that of your descendants.

Chapter Three

WRITE IT DOWN

*Write down the vision and inscribe it
clearly on tablets...
(Habakkuk 2:2, NASB)*

I MIGHT BE taking the above scripture out of context a bit, but I believe the principle is about writing down one's goals. The prophet Habakkuk was given a vision and God told him to write it down. God was clear that it would surely come to pass; even if it seemed delayed, it would happen.

The principle here is that there is power in writing something down and declaring it.

So my question to you is this: what do you want? Only you can answer this question. Do you want a nice home or a better job or to start your own business or to excel in your career? What would make a better life for your family?

Whatever it is you want, write it down.

A good place to do this is in a journal. I highly recommend journaling. It's a way to record your prayers, dreams, and goals... and remind yourself each day to be intentional about your goals. Most people live their lives in a random fashion, without direction, and hope that somehow the life they dream of will magically come to fruition.

The reality is that people only achieve their goals through focus, and writing down your goals each day and looking at them will help you stay focused. As you focus on your goals, you'll start to believe. Your goals will become a reality in your mind and change your paradigm. You will gain momentum as you move closer to those goals, day by day.

This may sound presumptuous, but let me ask you a few more questions. What if you could change anything in your life? What if you could start over? What if you could be or have anything you want? What would that look like?

Now, you may be in a very difficult situation at the moment, or you may have come from a harsh background. You may not be educated or qualified or skilled. You may believe that life won't ever get better for you or that you simply aren't one of the fortunate ones.

Let me assure you that it doesn't matter what your current situation is. God has given you a powerful tool: a mind that can think, believe, and make choices. Having the ability to choose is very powerful. You need to decide you want a better life… and then you must choose the life you want.

You are where you are because you choose to be there.

Now, you might argue with me. You may say your life is so bad that no one would ever choose what you're going through. But however difficult your situation, the hard truth is that you are choosing to stay there. If that wasn't true, you would be somewhere else.

Your circumstances may not change overnight, but I want to plant the seed of hope that they could change.

The first step is deciding what you want. What do you really want your life to look like? Write these dreams down in your journal. Date it and go back to it every day.

As you're thinking about this, let me encourage you to dream *big*. Our God is a big God and He will exceed your expectations.

Our lives are made up of many components, and each should be reflected in your journal. You'll want to include your spiritual life, family life, physical life, work life, and financial life. Make a table of columns and list your goals for each aspect of your life.

Here's what I want you to take away from this chapter: if you want to have abundance, wealth, financial freedom, or whatever term you want to call it, you need to be focused. You need to live intentionally, because wealth won't come to you by chance.

This goes for all the goals you have listed. Focus is key. Spend time with each goal. Pray about them, talk about them, and read books about them. Find other people who have the same desires and become friends with them. Become friends with people who have achieved what you're dreaming about and ask them to mentor you.

Decide every day to choose to live this life you're dreaming about. Be intentional. Your life will head in the direction of your thoughts. So stay focused. In order to take the needed steps in that direction, you can't afford to be sidetracked.

Chapter Four

PRINCIPLE OF INCREASE

> ...whoever gathers money
> little by little makes it grow.
> (Proverbs 13:11)

IN THE WORKSHOPS I hold for our staff and students at Grace Academy in Zambia, I usually start with two declarations.

The first is that the Bible is full of treasures and secrets to obtaining wealth. Ponder the words of Proverbs 25:2: *"It is the glory of God to conceal a matter; to search out a matter is the glory of kings."* Is it possible that the secrets of life, health, peace, and abundance are all hidden in plain sight in the Word of God? I would answer this with an emphatic, resounding *yes*.

My second declaration is that math is your friend. Even this is stated in the Word of God:

> *Suppose one of you wants to build a tower. Won't you first sit down and estimate the cost to see if you have enough money to complete it? For if you lay the foundation and are not able to finish it, everyone who sees it will ridicule you, saying, "This person began to build and wasn't able to finish."* (Luke 14:28–30)

If you were to read the whole of Luke 14, you would see that I'm taking this out of context, for Jesus is talking about the cost of following Him. However, there remains an important principle to take note of, and it's about counting the cost. This applies to everything we do. Some might say it's nothing more than budgeting, but I say it's more than that. It's understanding a variety of financial principles, such as percentages, averages, and risks.

Here's an example. When teaching these two declarations, I pose a question to the class: "If I offered you one million U.S. dollars or a magical dollar that doubled every day for thirty days, which would you take?" There's always a pause, a lull of silence as they think about it.

Almost everyone then says, "Give me the million dollars."

Once, though, a young woman told me that she would take the one dollar.

"Are you sure?" I asked.

"Yes."

"Why?"

She couldn't answer right away, but she looked around the class to see what everyone thought. Still she insisted that she would take the one dollar.

"Think about it," I then explained to the class. "One dollar will turn into two dollars after one day. Then four, then eight, then sixteen, then thirty-two, then sixty-four. After one week, it will only be 128 dollars. So are you sure you don't want one million dollars?"

With that, she relented and agreed with the crowd that taking the million dollars was the right thing.

I'll go back to the doubling dollar anecdote later, but first we need to address a huge lesson here. What happened in the class is the same thing happening to the majority of people in the world today. Most people follow the crowd without ever thinking whether they're right or wrong. My advice is simple: "Don't follow the crowd. Learn to think for yourself."

The second thing we need to talk about is the importance of learning to do math. Most people want instant gratification—they want a new vehicle, designer clothes, fancy coffees every day, and the fun, carefree lifestyle they see all around them. They want it now and don't take into account the cost of this lifestyle.

Believe me, this is an expensive lifestyle, as we'll see in the following chapters.

As implied by the title of this chapter, money will grow little by little when you save it. Learning to save some of your income from every paycheck and put it into an account you don't touch is a discipline that will payoff exponentially.

Most people in North America live beyond their means. In other words, they spend more than they earn.

Living within your means might sound like an elementary idea, especially if you're an experienced investor or businessperson, but it's a principle I wish I had learned earlier in my life. Many people struggle with this.

It is common in today's society not to be taught how to handle money. Perhaps, when you think about sharing this book with someone, a name immediately comes to mind—someone who could use some help in this area.

What I want to convey is that you don't need to be well-educated to be financially independent. Although owning a business or having a degree expedites the process of wealth, the good news is that it's more important to have the correct mindset. As a matter of fact, some of the wealthiest people I know are immigrants who can hardly speak English!

If you're struggling to make ends meet, working hard every week only to barely get by, just know that I was in the same situation. I wish someone had told me years ago what I'm sharing with you now. It is my earnest desire to help people experience abundance.

Let's go back to the question I posed earlier. How much is a dollar that's doubled thirty times? The answer: more than half a billion dollars!

$1 Doubled for 30 days	
Day 1	$1
Day 2	$2
Day 3	$4
Day 4	$8
Day 5	$16
Day 6	$32
Day 7	$64
Day 8	$128
Day 9	$256
Day 10	$512
Day 11	$1,024
Day 12	$2,048
Day 13	$4,096
Day 14	$8,192
Day 15	$16,384
Day 16	$32,768
Day 17	$65,536
Day 18	$131,072
Day 19	$262,144
Day 20	$524,288
Day 21	**$1,048,576**
Day 22	$2,097,152
Day 23	$4,194,304
Day 24	$8,383,608
Day 25	$16,777,216
Day 26	$33,554,432
Day 27	$67,108,864
Day 28	$134,217,728
Day 29	$268,435,456
Day 30	$536,870,912

If you were to add a bonus day, it would amount to over a billion dollars—that's one thousand times one million!

This exercise is meant to demonstrate how explosive exponential growth can be.

Another example I use is to bring a fifty-gallon drum into one of my classrooms. Employing an eyedropper, I drop one drop of water into the drum.

"This is a magic drop," I say to the class. "Just as with the dollar, it will double every minute. So at 11:01, the drop will become two drops. At 11:02, it will become four drops, and so on. Soon it will become one gallon. Then, a minute later, it will become two gallons. It is now eleven o'clock. At exactly twelve o'clock, the drum will be completely full."

I then pose another question to the class: "When will the drum be half full?"

Most of the class will answer, "11:30."

But in fact it will be half full at 11:59.

The point here is that it takes time for money to compound (grow). At first it will seem like very little is happening, but over time the growth will become explosive. This is the problem for most people. They are impatient. Most people spend frivolously. They don't give a second thought to spending five or ten dollars every morning on coffee and donuts, not realizing the power of those dollars to multiply. Not to mention going into debt for big ticket items.

We will continue with this theme in the coming chapters.

Creating wealth is about making good decisions—and the earlier you start, the more your money can grow through compound interest and wise investments.

However, I also want to point out that it is never too late to start. It is said that the best time to plant a tree is twenty years ago, and the second best time is right now. It's never too late to start making good financial decisions. For that matter, it's never too late to start taking care of your body or your mind or to learn new things like a new language or skill. Start today to have the amazing and abundant life of your dreams.

Chapter Five

POWER OF DOUBLING

*The one who had received the five talents
immediately went and did business with them,
and earned five more talents.*
(Matthew 25:16, NASB)

IF YOU READ the story in Matthew 25, you'll discover that it's about a king who went on a journey. But before he left, he entrusted three of his servants with large sums of money.

Each was given a different amount according to his ability. One was given five talents, the second was given two talents, and the third servant was given one talent.

For context, a talent is estimated to have been worth twenty years of a day laborer's wage.

The first and second servant invested the money, putting it to work. They doubled their master's money and gained a one hundred percent return.

The third servant, however, became afraid that he would lose the money. So he dug a hole and buried what had been entrusted to him.

After a long time, the master returned and settled the accounts. He was pleased with the first two men and how they had invested his funds. He praised them and rewarded them with even more. But he was greatly displeased with the third man and called him lazy. He took away what had been entrusted to this man, severely punished him, and then gave away the talent to the one who had originally been given five.

This might seem very unfair, but there is a biblical principle here to understand. Mark 4:25 puts it this way: *"Whoever has will be given more; whoever does not have, even what they have will be taken from them."*

Have you ever heard the saying "the rich keep getting richer and the poor, poorer"? Why do you think that is? I think it's because most wealthy people understand the worth of a dollar and how it grows, while most people who have not been taught this mindset are interested in instant gratification. Instant gratification translates into debt, bad financial decisions, bad spending habits, and a misunderstanding of basic financial principles.

When one has little, the financial stakes are even higher. They fear that the little they have will be taken from them.

There are many other gems of wisdom in this story that will help us understand certain financial principles. Notice that each servant was given different amounts, each according to his ability. What I have learned from this passage is not to look at what others have but to do the best with what I have.

Today, we use the word "talent" to describe one's ability, skill, and gifting. In any case, the story illustrates that God expects a return from whatever He has gifted us with, whether it's money, skills, leadership, or sphere of influence. We all have talents! The question is, how do we invest what He has given us? If we understand that the talents entrusted to us belong to the Master, our attitude towards money will be different from those who want to get wealthy for the sake of earning riches.

Being a wealthy believer should be about serving Him to whom we belong. This brings about the correct perspective about wealth and how to use it.

The other important thing I have noticed from this story is that the first two servants put the money to work. The Bible doesn't say that they themselves went out and worked. Instead they invested the money; the money did the work. This is important to understand: once you spend your hard-earned dollar, it is no longer able to grow for you.

AMAZING ABUNDANCE

While teaching a financial class with my staff at Grace Academy in Zambia, the subject turned to another subject: "Where do you keep your money?" I asked.

I got many confused looks.

Finally someone answered: "The bank."

"In what kind of account?"

Again, the confused looks.

It turned out that the students had placed their money in either a savings or checking account. In some cases, they hid their money in their homes.

The kicker is that their money was in the national currency, the kwacha. That year, the kwacha went from an exchange rate of roughly ten kwacha per U.S. dollar to twenty kwacha per U.S. dollar. By the end of the year, their hard-earned money was worth half of what it had been at the start of the year. In addition, the price of goods had greatly increased. I explained that if they had put their money in a U.S. dollar account, at the very least they would have been protected from this massive inflation.

At the end of the class, I went back to review the two core statements I had made at the beginning: there is hidden treasure in the Bible, and math is your friend. If you aren't good at math, take the time to go online and learn. You can engage many free programs to improve your knowledge of math, and especially percentages.

In North America, our money gets eaten away by inflation, interest paid on debt, and other hidden costs. As a society, we are deeply in debt and don't understand how interest rates work for or against us. Consider where you put your hard-earned money.

I once spoke to a young man named KC who told me how broke he was. He complained that he didn't make enough money and that his company should take better care of its employees. This puzzled me, because he made good money in the construction industry. He was single and had few expenses.

So I asked him how he spent his money. It turned out that he owed money on his truck, went out every weekend, ate often in restaurants, and smoked.

KC was taken aback when I told him that he should be able to be very wealthy based on what he earned.

"How's that?" he asked.

"Well, tell me how much you spend on cigarettes each day."

"Thirteen dollars."

I explained that if he were to instead invest those thirteen dollars a day, which would equal $400 per month, putting it into a mutual fund with an average annual return of ten percent and left it there... then he would retire with more than a million dollars. After all, he was only in his twenties.

"Not only that," I added, "but by quitting smoking, you will live longer and healthier!"

It may surprise you to learn that creating wealth is more about making good decisions than working hard.

Assuming an average annual rate of return of ten percent, his money would double every seven years in that mutual fund.[2] In addition, he would earn dividends which could be reinvested and help his money to grow even faster. If it were a mutual fund connected to a registered retirement fund (in Canada) or an IRA or 401k (in the U.S.), he would get back a portion in tax returns which, if reinvested, would also speed the rate of growth.

Many companies offer their employees a matching contribution plan (401k) up to a certain amount. If your company offers this, you should maximize your contribution because you will have doubled your money from the get-go!

This is the simplest way to at least get to a comfortable retirement. If you were to have your monthly contributions automatically deducted

---

[2] Use the Rule of 72, a mathematical formula used to figure out how long your investment will take to double. Divide 72 by the rate of return. In this case, it is 72 divided by 10, which equals 7.2 years. For more information on the Rule of 72, visit: Will Kenton, "Rule of 72," *Investopedia*. Date of access: July 19, 2022 (www.investopedia.com/terms/r/ruleof72.asp).

from your checking account into your investment account, you wouldn't even have to think about it. It would be automatic.

Make the commitment today to make an appointment with a financial advisor, your bank, or your employer to start your RRSP, IRA, or 401k deductions at your earliest convenience.

The only willpower or discipline you need is to start this process in the first place. KC got very excited about this and started investing his four hundred dollars that month. No one had ever told him how to invest, or talked to him about being financially independent. He was so excited about what he'd learned that he actually quit smoking! He not only got excited about wealth, he got excited about health.

After a while, KC came back to me and asked, "What else can I do to make my money grow?"

"Okay," I said. "Let's take a look at your financial situation, starting with your debt."

Chapter Six

THE TRAP OF DEBT

...the borrower is slave to the lender.
(Proverbs 22:7)

KC, LIKE MANY people, had fallen into the trap of debt. He was very honest with me and openly shared about his struggles.

His biggest debt was his truck. I explained that far too many people have car loans that eat into their wages so that they have very little, if any, money at the end of the month.

He was paying more than $500 a month and still had a few years to go. I explained to him that the moment he had driven the truck off the lot, it had depreciated by twenty percent... and that it had continued to depreciate with every year and every mile and every ding. He still owed more than $20,000.

His face said it all. It was like it was begging me, *Please, not my truck*.

I knew he loved his truck, but I explained to him that the reason most people aren't wealthy has nothing to do with how much they earn. Instead it has to do with making poor decisions and living beyond their needs.

"If you're willing to make the tough decisions now, in ten years you will be able to go into that dealership and buy your dream truck with cash. My advice to you is to sell the truck, use that money to pay off the outstanding debt on it, then pay off your credit card."

He had about $4,000 in credit card debt.

"Then you should have enough left over to buy yourself a small commuter car," I said. "Here's the good news. If you do this, you will be saving well over $10,000 every year when you add together the money you've saved from quitting smoking, the savings from your truck payments, and the interest charges on your credit card."

This was $10,000 that he could invest, putting it to work for him.

Now, remember the power of compound interest and how money multiplies. This principle works both ways, for you and against you. When you're in debt, the reality of high interest rates means that debt increases rapidly. The average cost of a major credit card is 18.5 percent—which is huge. This is how so many people get entangled in an endless cycle of debt. They live paycheck to paycheck with absolutely no backup plan in case of emergency.

KC walked away with very little expression on his face, but I could tell he was in deep thought. I think he had been expecting some kind of magical formula to achieve wealth. I knew that he loved his truck and that this would be a painful decision for him. I hoped he would make the right choice.

A couple of weeks later, he called me. With excitement in his voice, he said, "Hey, I want you to see my new ride."

A half-hour later, while raking leaves out in the yard, I saw him pull up in his ten-year-old beater car. I almost laughed out loud. KC was a really cool dude, and driving around in his truck had really suited him. It had made him look like a guy who had money.

But that's the problem. So many people look like they have money, driving fancy cars, wearing expensive clothing, and spending too much on entertainment. It reminds me of another biblical saying: *"One person pretends to be rich, yet has nothing; another pretends to be poor, yet has great wealth"* (Proverbs 13:7).

Now KC looked like he was on his way to being the latter.

I smiled at him when he got out of the car. "I didn't know if you would do it," I said. "I'm really proud of you! And I just thought of another source of savings you realized. With the cost of fuel and the cheaper insurance for this car, I bet you're saving more than $400 every month."

That was an additional $4,800 a year that would go to work for him.

At the start of the chapter, I quoted Proverbs 22:7, which tells us that *"the borrower is slave to the lender."* This is absolutely true. People will spend a large portion of their lives paying off debt. As a matter of fact, many people go to their graves in debt. Is that the way you want to live your life, or are you willing to make some sacrifices now to later attain the financial freedom of your dreams?

Another biblical passage describes the urgency of getting out of debt:

My son, if you have put up security for your neighbor, if you have shaken hands in pledge for a stranger, you have been trapped by what you said, ensnared by the words of your mouth. So do this, my son, to free yourself, since you have fallen into your neighbor's hands: go—to the point of exhaustion—and give your neighbor no rest! Allow no sleep to your eyes, no slumber to your eyelids. Free yourself, like a gazelle from the hand of the hunter, like a bird from the snare of the fowler. (Proverbs 6:1–5)

The writer here talks about guaranteeing a debt for another, but I think the same principle applies to our own debts. We need to make whatever sacrifices we must in order to get out of debt.

Here's a simple rule: if you don't have the cash to buy something, don't buy it.

KC was able to get himself out of debt with little sacrifice compared to someone who has a family and children and a mortgage. For those who have a family, it will be a lot more difficult but even more urgent to get out of debt. It will take sacrifice and determination.

Let's look at some strategies to eliminate your debt. I would advise you to start by tackling your smallest debt while making minimum payments on the others. The smallest debt should be the easiest and quickest to get rid of. The psychology behind this is that you start with success and build momentum as you realize more and more success.

However, you must also consider the interest rates and amount of each debt. In some cases, you would want to pay down the debt with the highest interest rate. For example, interest rates for a new car loan are about 5.5 percent while credit card rates are about 18.5 percent. Remember, math is your friend.

Another thing you can do is call your debtors, negotiate a payment plan, and automate it so that it comes out of your account on its own. The trick here is to stick to a budget, and as you knock off one debt that payment can be applied to the next. Finishing one debt doesn't mean you have extra money to spend; it just means you have to keep going.

I know people who have maxed out multiple credit cards and owe money on everything from furniture and appliances to cars. If this describes your situation, I would suggest getting professional help with a debt counselor. It may be embarrassing to take this step, but this would be an act of courage. Trying to better yourself and your family is something to be proud of.

We live in a time when most people have never been taught how to handle money, and they are relentlessly bombarded by every sort of media to buy, buy, buy. They're enticed with all kinds of loan plans—"Don't pay for a year"—and other incentives that businesses use to get you hooked and paying for years to come.

I especially urge young couples, as they start their married life, to avoid debt. The first ten years of marriage is a financial struggle, especially if you have young children, as you try to establish your career and buy your first home. Adding debt to the equation only introduces an enormous amount of stress.

You will be tempted to take on debt, but make up your minds to sacrifice now so that you will have the financial freedom you dream of in the future.

Here are some ways you can save (a lot of) money.

- Learn to cook. Don't eat out, or do it very rarely.
- Bring your lunch to work.
- Bike to work.
- Learn to live with only one vehicle.
- Buy used items in good condition (right off the bat, you save the sales tax and usually fifty percent off the retail value).
- Don't buy coffee, donuts, etc. on your way to work or from a vending machine.
- Cancel your subscriptions.
- If you live in an apartment, share your internet with your neighbor.
- Instead of going out on the weekends, have friends come over and ask them to bring some food and drinks.
- If you're living on your own, get a roommate. If you're married and have an extra bedroom, rent it out or rent out the garage.

If you think creatively, you can find ways to save hundreds of dollars each month. Think of the savings you can realize by cutting out needless expenses. Taking these steps will certainly be a sacrifice.

Why would you do all this?

For me and my wife Susan, we wanted our own house for our kids to grow up in. Then, after we bought it, we still needed to sacrifice because our mortgage payment was high. However, the sacrifice has certainly paid off. Since we bought our home, the value of it has more than quadrupled! I will share more on buying a home later.

So what is your motivation to keep you focused and committed?

To build wealth, you'll need to understand that there are steps to follow. The very first step is to save a portion of what you earn. Most financial advisors say that you should save at least ten percent.

The most important thing you can take away from this book is this: you will *never* have abundance or wealth if you spend more than you make, or spend all that you make. By definition, abundance means having a surplus. Being in debt means you have a deficit.

Make the decision right now to save a portion of your earnings. To start with, you should build a savings account that will serve as an emergency fund. The goal here is to have three months of living expenses put aside for emergencies. But this isn't a vacation fund! It is only to be used in case of emergency. For example, a car breakdown.

After you build your emergency fund, you need an investment account in which your money can grow. I'll share more about this later.

The second step is to say no to debt. You cannot build wealth if you keep giving away your hard-earned money to the credit card company or the bank.

Chapter Seven

MULTIPLE SOURCES OF INCOME

*Sow your seed in the morning, and at evening let
your hands not be idle, for you do not know
which will succeed, whether this or that,
or whether both will do equally well.*
(Ecclesiastes 11:6)

ONE OF THE biggest traps in life is comfort. It's a smooth paved highway to poverty. Millions of people come home after work and turn on the TV, sitting there for hours each night and wasting their precious time. Others are addicted to video games and again waste hours upon hours of their time and mental energy. These people are often the same ones complaining that they can't get ahead, that they don't earn enough, that they're broke and have so much debt. It seems to them that life is so unfair.

TV and video games themselves are not the problem. There are times when I want to watch a movie or a ballgame as well. I'm not saying you shouldn't watch TV. I *am* saying that you shouldn't let it be your master.

If you look at people who are successful in the business world and those who are wealthy, you'll see that they share certain habits that made them that way. One habit is to be on the lookout for opportunities. Another is to always have a side hustle. They come home from work and go right back to work. It might be something simple like reading about investments and studying how money works. It might be selling things they've made or providing a service they're good at.

In the previous chapter, I talked about how Susan and I sacrificed to buy a house. During the day I was a bricklayer, and in the evening I worked in a warehouse. On the weekends I framed walls in the basement and built an apartment to rent to help with our mortgage payments. Susan stayed home with our young children and started babysitting our neighbors' kids while their mothers went to work.

Those were exhausting times for us. When I look back, I don't know how we did it. But we worked hard, paid down our mortgage, and built equity. We were able to raise our kids with love and provide them with all the things kids need to have a happy childhood. We earned extra income to allow us to take vacations and outings. We enjoyed camping, fishing, and team sports. We were able to make incredible memories.

The kids never realized how much we had to sacrifice, but Susan and I always looked for ways to save money so we could provide the life we wanted for our kids. This was before we went into the ministry. As a matter of fact, we wouldn't have been able to go into the ministry had we not had a house and a certain amount of funds. When we first went on the mission field, we rented out our house and put our belongings in our basement for storage.

The takeaway here is that it's a good idea to have alternate sources of income to help you achieve your dream. With today's technology, opportunities abound. If you aren't tech-savvy, I'm sure you have a talent someone is willing to pay for. Do you like to fish? Maybe you can tie flies in the evenings and sell them online or at your local sporting goods store. If you're athletic, you could look into being a personal trainer. Can you design websites? Are you a graphic artist? Have you thought about online sales?

Here is an inventory of ideas to earn some income on the side. Beyond these, there are countless ways to make money.

- Mechanical repairs
- Renovations
- Painting

- Typing services
- Janitorial services
- Tutoring
- Editing services
- Tailoring services
- Delivery services
- Personal trainer

What do you love to do? Do it well enough so that people are willing to pay you for it.

I want to end this chapter with a scripture that reminds me of my wife, who has always been diligent with our money, time, and well-being. As you read this, see if you can count how many sources of income this woman had.

> *A wife of noble character who can find? She is worth far more than rubies. Her husband has full confidence in her and lacks nothing of value. She brings him good, not harm, all the days of her life. She selects wool and flax and works with eager hands. She is like the merchant ships, bringing her food from afar. She gets up while it is still night; she provides food for her family and portions for her female servants. She considers a field and buys it; out of her earnings she plants a vineyard. She sets about her work vigorously; her arms are strong for her tasks. She sees that her trading is profitable, and her lamp does not go out at night. In her hand she holds the distaff and grasps the spindle with her fingers. She opens her arms to the poor and extends her hands to the needy. When it snows, she has no fear for her household; for all of them are clothed in scarlet. She makes coverings for her bed; she is clothed in fine linen and purple. Her husband is respected at the city gate, where he takes his seat among the elders of the land. She makes linen garments and sells them, and supplies the merchants with*

sashes. She is clothed with strength and dignity; she can laugh at the days to come. She speaks with wisdom, and faithful instruction is on her tongue. She watches over the affairs of her household and does not eat the bread of idleness. Her children arise and call her blessed; her husband also, and he praises her: "Many women do noble things, but you surpass them all." Charm is deceptive, and beauty is fleeting; but a woman who fears the Lord is to be praised. (Proverbs 31:10–30)

Chapter Eight

MAKING MONEY WHILE YOU SLEEP

*...whether he sleeps or gets up,
the seed sprouts and grows...*
(Mark 4:27)

IMAGINE, IF YOU will, making money while you sleep. Isn't that an amazing thought? I want to assure you that it's possible. In fact, it's called passive income—and it's the way that wealthy people make their money.

Think of an owner of rental properties. Every month, he collects the rent from all his tenants. Nowadays he doesn't even have to go out and physically collect the rent, as it's electronically deposited into his account. He can be away on vacation in the tropics and the money still comes through.

Now that's my idea of passive income!

There are many ways to have passive income, including dividends, royalties, subscriptions, leases, licenses to use your brand or product, and rentals. However, the most common source is investing in the stock market.

Earlier, I mentioned that there are a number of steps you can take to build wealth. The first is to save a portion of what you earn, and the second is to eliminate debt. The third step is to invest your money where it will grow.

Now think about this. It's important that you take care of the second step before you start to invest, because you'd be hard-pressed to find any investment that consistently pays the 18.5 percent a person would otherwise be paying their credit card company. Remember to make math your friend.

In my opinion, mutual funds are the easiest and probably safest way to enter the world of investing, especially if it's a retirement fund through your place of employment.

So let's say that you're saving a portion of your wages, that you've paid off your debt and started a retirement account. A good idea now would be to talk to a financial advisor about how to invest your money. Money that's left in the bank won't grow. It'll be eaten away by inflation and fees.

Most people believe that only those with a lot of expertise and money can buy stocks. Nothing could be further from the truth, but you do need to educate yourself. Start by getting some books or doing some research on the internet. Learn the terminology and the dos and don'ts. Seek the help of a financial advisor or professional wealth management firm.

Secondly, look for a mentor. Find someone who is doing well and has experience. Look for someone who has a successful track record. Ask them questions like who they use to help them manage their investments and how they would advise someone who's just starting out.

The thought of investing might seem like a daunting task, but let me encourage you by telling you the story of Curtis "Wall Street" Caroll. In 1996, at the age of seventeen, Caroll was convicted of murder and robbery. He's currently serving a life sentence. He entered prison illiterate, but by the age of twenty he had taught himself to read and write. Then he taught himself how to invest in the stock market. He's an amazing young man who has taken it upon himself to teach other inmates how to build wealth and become productive citizens.[3]

---

[3] Curtis Caroll, "How I Learned to Read—and Trade Stocks—in Prison," *YouTube*. May 18, 2017 (https://www.youtube.com/watch?v=F89eycANUrQ).

AMAZING ABUNDANCE

Here's the thing: if a man serving time in prison can teach himself how to read and write, and then how to invest in stocks, so can you. You're (probably) not in jail, so you have no excuse.

It has never been easier to invest in the stock market than right now because of all the technology available to us. You can get an investment account with your bank and start investing with your phone or computer from the comfort of your home.

Here are some questions to think about first. What do you spend money on each day, or each week? What kind of smartphone do you use? What kind of technology are you interested in? What types of recreational activities are you interested in? What products do you use on a regular basis? What if instead of purchasing these items or services, you abstained for a while and bought stocks in those companies instead? I'm not saying you should buy stock in all your favorite companies, but pick a few.

Take a look at a graph of the Dow Jones index for the last ten years, or look at a graph showing the stock performances of one of your favorite companies. What was their stock worth ten years ago? Many big companies were penny stocks ten years ago, meaning that their stock could have been bought for less than a dollar per share. Now these companies' shares are worth hundreds of dollars. What if you had bought back then?

In the same way that KC started putting $400 into a retirement fund every month, you can start an investment account and start buying shares. The important thing to remember is that this is a long-term commitment. It requires discipline. So make up your mind to stop wasting money frivolously and start investing in your future.

Think of your money as seed. The seed you plant today will produce a crop yielding much, much more than what was planted. It will take time, and at first you won't see anything happen. You might think it was a waste, especially if your investment goes down. It's important that you know that stocks will fluctuate. They will go down, then up, then back down. But over time, you will notice an upward trend.

Now consider an analogy. A farmer might sow his seed and then experience a drought, or perhaps too much rain. Every farmer has good years and bad years. But whatever hardship might come in a season, a farmer would never harvest his crop early. That would be like pulling out your investments before they've had a chance to grow to their full potential.

In the same way, invest for the long term and don't let the fluctuation of the market scare you. The market will fluctuate. Think ten years or more down the road. Think of a company that's on top of their competition and that's likely to be strong in ten years' time. That's the type of company you want to invest in.

Here's the takeaway from this chapter: make the commitment to talk to someone, preferably a professional financial advisor or wealth manager, about investing in the stock market.

The first time I talked to a wealth management firm, I was told that I needed $100,000 to start an account with them. I was so discouraged that I didn't invest until years later.

Never accept an answer like that. You can invest with only one hundred dollars, so don't be dismayed if at first they look down on you for not having a lot of money.

Here's another gem from the Bible: *"Ask and it will be given to you; seek and you will find; knock and the door will be opened to you"* (Matthew 7:7). Be persistent.

Also, meditate on this passage of scripture:

This is what the kingdom of God is like. A man scatters seed on the ground. Night and day, whether he sleeps or gets up, the seed sprouts and grows, though he does not know how. All by itself the soil produces grain—first the stalk, then the head, then the full kernel in the head. As soon as the grain is ripe, he puts the sickle to it, because the harvest has come. (Mark 4:26–29)

Think about where you want to invest your money, your time, your love, and ultimately your faith. Whatever you sow will come back to you manyfold.

Chapter Nine
GOOD DEBT

*Do not be one who shakes hands in
pledge or puts up security for debts;
if you lack the means to pay...*
(Proverbs 22:26–27)

IS THERE EVER a time to go into debt? To me, the above scripture holds the key: yes, if you have the means to pay. It's not a sin to go into debt, but it is bondage—or at the very least, a burden. You need to carefully consider your reasons for doing so.

As I wrote in an earlier chapter, Susan and I had a dream to buy a house in which to raise our family. In those days, people used to say, "Houses are so expensive now. I don't know how young people can ever afford them."

Guess what? People are still saying this.

How did we do it? We made the decision to focus on this goal, and we did what we had to do to get there. It's the very same thing you will have to do.

The cost to buy a house has continued to go up every year. Most people cannot afford to buy a house outright. Most people are hard-pressed just to come up with the twenty percent down-payment.

I realize that I just finished warning of the perils of debt, but if there was ever a good debt, it would be the mortgage for your own home. The reason that a mortgage is considered good debt is that the value of your home is very likely to appreciate. This is unlike a credit card purchase or car loan, where the purchased item always depreciates in value. In that scenario, you'll end up paying more for it in the long run as it loses its value.

The alternative to buying your own home would be to rent a house or apartment, in the process making someone else wealthy. The reality is that unless you're living with your parents, you'll be paying either rent or a mortgage payment. Both will be about the same amount. However, when paying rent you walk away without an asset, even if you rented the same place for decades. By owning a home and paying the mortgage every month, you'll eventually pay it off and be worth hundreds of thousands of dollars—or a lot more.

In the beginning, gathering enough money for a down-payment is difficult, and perhaps making those early monthly payments will be a financial stretch.

For me and my wife, what was really important about purchasing a home was that it would be ours. We wouldn't have a landlord telling us that we couldn't decorate a certain way or that we couldn't have pets—or even worse, that we were being evicted.

Besides the security, owning a home, to me, is far more tangible than owning stocks. Why? Because you live in it. Some people say that owning a home is a liability unless it's making money for you, but I would argue that it's one of the best investments you can make in terms of personal security and for the sake of your investment.

Let's suppose that you purchased a home for $400,000 and put down $80,000 for a down-payment, which in this case is twenty percent. If you had used that money to purchase stocks and earned ten percent, you would have made $8,000. However, if your home goes up in value ten percent, you don't just earn ten percent on the down-payment you started with. The whole value of the house goes up in value by ten percent, which is equal to $40,000! As you pay down your principle—in other words, the amount you owe—your equity will grow. You can look at it as forced savings, since your net worth goes up each month you pay your mortgage.

If you rent out a portion of your house, like a basement suite or the garage, the renter is actually paying at least part of your mortgage.

There are also tax benefits to owning a home, as you can write off your mortgage interest payment, especially if you have a home business.

Of course, owning a home isn't for everyone. There are many considerations to take into account. For example, it may not work if you have a job that requires you to frequently relocate. It also may not be an option if your budget can't handle the added expense of maintenance. The workload and skillset needed to maintain the home may also be a barrier.

But the point I want to reinforce is that home ownership is an option you should consider carefully when deciding what's best for your family.

Even if you don't want to buy real estate to live in, it's still a good option to invest in real estate for the purpose of earning rental income or forming an REIT (real estate investment trust). An REIT company owns and usually operates commercial properties ranging from hotels and resorts to apartment buildings and shopping malls. The great thing about REITs is that they pay dividends on a regular basis, which is a form of passive income. Talk to your financial advisor about REITs.

What I want you to carefully consider after reading these last few chapters is how to make your money grow. If you're trying to become financially independent, your money needs to grow and work for you.

You might agree with everything you've just read, but unless you make a commitment to make the necessary changes to live an abundant life, nothing will change for you. Einstein said it best when he defined insanity as doing the same thing over and over again, expecting a different result.

Chapter Ten

POSSIBILITIES AND PROBABILITIES

*All things are possible for
the one who believes.*
(Mark 9:23, NASB)

ONE DAY I had a pleasant conversation with Mapalo, one of our senior students in Zambia. We were talking about in life in general when I asked him about his plans for when he finished school. He told me that he was planning to be a doctor.

Usually I'm not as blunt as I was with Mapalo that day. I prefer to speak encouragingly to our students, but this time I straight-out told him that it wasn't going to happen.

He looked at me, shocked. I could almost see the wheels turning in his head. He was likely thinking, *But you told us we can do anything, that we can be anything.*

At that time, five of our graduates were enrolled in medical school and a few others enrolled in nursing. I think Mapalo thought he, too, would just breeze right on in there.

I asked him why he thought he would be accepted into medical school, since I knew his marks were mediocre to poor. Although he was a great kid, he always struggled through school. His answer was that he wanted to have a nice car and lots of money.

This answer was void of passion. He had no desire to help others. It demonstrated his ignorance of what it takes to be a doctor.

"Let me tell you about three boys your age," I said. "The first one is named Mike. Mike's father is a surgeon at the local hospital. Not only that, but he's also a professor at the medical college. His mother is a doctor, too, with her own practice. All his life, Mike has heard stories around the dinner table about fascinating medical cases and procedures. All his parents' friends are in the medical profession, so Mike grew up immersed in that world. He dreamed of one day following in the footsteps of his parents and bringing healing to hurting people. His marks at school are excellent and he thrives in the sciences. He knows all the right people and has the best references.

"What do you think is the probability of him not only getting into medical school but becoming a great doctor? I would say it's a slam dunk!

"Then there's Jack. Jack comes from a middle-class family and loves sports. He is one of the star athletes at his high school. He is a popular kid and has lots of friends.

"One day after winning an important game, a reporter asks Jack what he's going to do after high school. His answer is that he wants to be a doctor and the reporter runs with the story. After that, he tells everyone that he's going to be a doctor. He loves watching medical dramas on TV and thinks it so cool that doctors get to hang out with beautiful nurses all day long. Jack's grades are average, though, and besides his idea of hanging out with nurses, he has no passion for the medical profession.

"What do you think is the probability of Jack getting into medical school? I would say very poor.

"Now consider Jorge, from an immigrant family. His parents own a restaurant and work long hours every day. English is his second language and school is a struggle for him. When he was about twelve years old, his baby sister had massive seizures and was rushed to the hospital and ended up on life support. The doctors frantically worked to save her. One brilliant young doctor figured out what was wrong and saved her life.

"From that day forward, Jorge has wanted to be a doctor. In high school, he works extra hard to get good grades and pays attention to the sciences. He has a dream to be a doctor, but he doesn't know how he's ever going to manage it.

"One day, Jorge thinks to make an appointment to see his family doctor. He phones the office and the receptionist asks the reason for his appointment.

"'Oh, there's nothing wrong,' he says. 'I just want to talk to Dr. Garcia.'

"'I'm sorry," she answers. 'You can't have an appointment just to talk to the doctor.'

But he keeps phoning every day and asking for the same thing. After about two weeks of this, the receptionist tells the doctor about Jorge's calls. Since Dr. Garcia followed up on Jorge's sister during her recovery, he knows Jorge and the family.

"'Give him an appointment,' says Dr. Garcia. He's curious as to what Jorge wants to talk about.

"The following week, Jorge gets to meet with the doctor and explains his dream of going into the medical field as well as his insecurities and questions about what he needs to do to make it happen. As he listens, Dr. Garcia is very impressed and comes up with many suggestions for Jorge, including extracurricular activities and volunteering at the local hospital.

"Jorge is very happy to follow all the doctor's advice. Soon he enrolls in night classes and volunteers at the local hospital, where he becomes familiar with the doctors and staff. He learns the terminology and the inner workings of the hospital. He walks around in his scrubs imagining that one day he will wear a stethoscope around his neck.

"Jorge graduates with honors. He receives many references from Dr. Garcia and the doctors at the hospital. He even wins a few scholarships.

"What do you think is the probability of Jorge getting into medical school? I would say it's about the same as Mike's: a slam dunk! Jorge had to overcome many obstacles, including the fact that English was his second language. He also had to work extra hard at school. He didn't have the help in his studies that Mike did. It was always possible for Jorge to be a doctor, but it wasn't probable. However, Jorge's efforts led to him qualifying himself, making the likelihood of him becoming a doctor very probable!"

Then I asked Mapalo which of these boys he was most like—Mike, Jack, or Jorge.

He understood my point. "Jack."

That was about two years ago. I met with Mapalo recently and he told me that his dream is now to be the first person in his family to graduate from college. He's upgrading his marks by taking courses and will soon be enrolling in college. He is qualifying himself for bigger and better things and I am so proud of him!

I would like to encourage you that it is very possible for you to have the financial freedom and wealth you dream about. However, you need to qualify yourself, just like Jorge and Mapalo.

Anything is possible for you, but is it probable? You decide.

Chapter Eleven

PERSISTENCE AND VISON

My people perish for lack of vision.
(Proverbs 29:18, paraphrased)

ONE DAY PATRICIA, our director of education, came to my door to discuss a school matter. After the discussion, she said to me, "John, I would like to show you the plans for the house I'm building."

"Oh," I said, curious to see these plans. "I didn't know you were building a house."

Patricia is a widow and has endured many struggles in her life. She lives next door to us at our staff housing at Grace Academy.

A few minutes later, she returned with the drawings in hand. I was astonished to see that she had actual architectural drawings. Most people in the townships built homes without plans. These were simple homes with bricks made of clay dug out from the ground.

Looking over the drawings, I could clearly see that this would be a modern home. The plans called for concrete blocks.

"Patricia, you're building a duplex!" I explained in excitement.

"Yes. I'll be renting out both sides."

Wow! I was so impressed. "Where did you get the idea to do this?"

"From you. I was listening to you talk to the students and thought, 'I can do this!'"

Patricia, like most people in Zambia, planned to build her home in stages as she earned enough money. Most people don't get mortgages in Zambia because the interest rates are too high. It would be finished within a few years and earn her passive income.

In the meantime, prices for lots have increased tremendously in Ndola so her net worth continues to grow.

Another couple we know, Shillah and Akson, has been working for Seeds of Hope for six years, Shillah as a housekeeper and Akson as one of our guards. Both have a great work ethic and continually try to improve themselves in everything they do. We are so impressed with this couple. They are remarkable.

Before they came to Seeds of Hope, it was a struggle for them to feed their family and find shelter. Most of the time Akson would do "piecework," which was temporary and mostly consisted of farm labor during the planting and harvest season. They have seven children, although one passed away at the age of six months. Paying school fees in Zambia is very expensive and their children haven't always been able to go to school.

However, since starting work at Seeds of Hope, their children are able to attend Grace Academy, and they are doing extremely well. The children value education and, like their parents, show an excellent work ethic. They are very grateful for the opportunities they have been given.

Even though both Shillah and Akson have steady employment at Grace Academy, life wasn't easy for them at first. They lived in a two-room brick home made out of clay dug from the ground, with a dirt floor and no running water. They lived rent-free in exchange for the whole family working the fields of the landowner. They walked two hours to get to work at Grace Academy, after which they'd put in a full day of labor, then walk two hours home and work the fields in the evening.

Working the fields is done with a hand hoe and is extremely laborious. Besides the physical difficulties, the couple also endured emotional upheavals. The previous year, they noticed their youngest child, six-month-old Gift, having trouble with his left eye. Upon visiting the clinic, they were referred to an ophthalmologist who diagnosed the eye as having cancer. Within a few days, the eye was removed.

This was an extremely emotional and taxing time for the family. At one point, Shillah collapsed in the hospital, stressed about what would happen to her child. But they continued working throughout the ordeal. Seeds of Hope paid for the surgeries and medical care and encouraged the couple.

Because it's difficult to feed three hundred people a day with inflation running rampant, our ministry started an agriculture project during this time to become self-sustaining. We started with growing chickens and fish—and aloe vera, to generate an income—so that we could control costs. Having a farm on site ensures the children can enjoy a high protein diet and good nutrition, which is especially important for children who are HIV positive.

We hired a North American couple to manage the farm. However, it has always been our intent to empower nationals. So because of their tremendous work ethic and love for working the soil, we hired Shillah and Akson to serve as intern farming managers, with the goal that they would one day manage the whole operation.

They now live in a modern house with running water and electricity. They don't have to walk for four hours a day. They have time for their children. They are able to learn modern agriculture and get ahead financially.

Akson is in the process of getting his driver's license, and he's also learning to operate farm machinery. With their earnings, they have already bought a lot and have begun to build a home they will rent out, creating another source of income for them. Eventually this will be their retirement home.

Although Shillah and Akson did attend one of my workshops, they were far on their way to making a better life for themselves by that time. I hope that I was a small encouragement to them.

Honestly, I would say they were more of an encouragement to me. They could have easily accepted their lot in life, but instead they chose to strive for better things for their family.

I write this to demonstrate how working towards your vision, with determination and passion, not letting obstacles stop you, will get results. Everyone I know who works towards a goal like Akson and Shillah soon discovers that they are able to far exceed what they imagined for themselves.

Chapter Twelve

CHOOSE TO BELIEVE

*Therefore, I say to you, all things for which you
pray and ask, believe that you have received
them, and they will be granted to you.*
(Mark 11:24, NASB)

THIS IS PROBABLY the most important chapter of the book. All the others can be understood, for the most part, with nothing more than one's natural mind. Save your money. Stay out of debt. Learn to invest. Persevere. We all understand these things.

But this chapter will require faith—not only that, but it will stretch and grow your faith.

God operates in the unseen spiritual sphere, unbound by time or space. His resources are unlimited.

We tend to think that there's a limit to how much money is out there. We think of the available money in the world like a pie, and there are only so many pieces. Therefore, in order for you to have a bigger piece, someone else will have to settle for a smaller piece.

This kind of thinking causes competition, strife, jealousy, and insecurity. God doesn't operate this way. His abundance is more than enough for everyone. It never runs out—ever!

I want to reiterate something we discussed back in Chapter Two. The way we think is shaped by our experiences, including our failures, and what we've been told. Fear and memories of failure limit us. These thoughts run continually in our subconscious minds like a computer program; they become our norm, our reality, the way we live our lives.

Indeed, neuroscientists say that ninety-five percent of our daily living is done using our subconscious mind.[4] In other words, we live on autopilot. This means that we interpret everything around us based on a program running in our mind, and our reality and feelings are based on that program.

So here's the key question: if our reality is based on how we think and how we think is based on a subconscious program of our past experiences, what would happen if we changed the program?

Do not conform to the pattern of this world, but be transformed by the renewing of your mind. Then you will be able to test and approve what God's will is—his good, pleasing and perfect will. (Romans 12:2)

The Bible tells us to renew our minds, and if God tells us to renew our mind, then it's not only possible but necessary. We are not to let the philosophy of the world, the circumstances around us, or our past experiences dictate how we think and live. We get to continually choose how we think, see the world, and react to circumstances.

So let's cast out the doubts and limitations of the past. Let's start believing for better things.

In a previous chapter, we read about Jorge, who walked around in his scrubs imagining that one day he would wear a stethoscope around his neck. He could see himself as a doctor. He could see himself doing his rounds, talking to patients, and prescribing medication. He then put himself in a position where he can actually experience the hospital. He put himself right in the middle of one, surrounding himself with his future reality.

To walk in faith means to take action believing that what you've prayed for is going to happen. You don't need to know how to accomplish it, but you need to see yourself exactly where you dream of being. Maybe you need to visualize yourself in the job or business

---

[4] Dr. Caroline Leaf, *Switch on Your Brain* (Ada, MI: Baker Books, 2013), 125, 135.

you want. Or it could be your dream home, the place where you will raise your children.

What is it you want? Dream about it. Write it down. Start to live it in your mind. Imagine how it would feel like to live in that reality.

Here is the supernatural aspect of wealth. In my experience, the best approach is to start doing all the things you are able to do... and then watch. God will show up in the most incredible way. He will put people in your path, people you don't even know yet. These people can help you and open doors. Opportunities you never knew existed will suddenly show up. He will arrange circumstances you would have thought impossible. Things will fall into place in the most miraculous way.

Here are a few things that happened to Susan and me as we began our journey of faith.

In 1997, we wanted to go to Thailand to work at the Agape Home for HIV/AIDS-affected or -infected orphans. We had helped start this home and wanted to go see it.

So we made plans to travel as a family for three months. In those days, we were able to book our flights through a travel agent and didn't have to pay until a couple of weeks before our departure. The cost for our family's airfare was about $10,000, not to mention that I would have to take three months off work. We had no idea where the money would come from. We had a mortgage payment, many expenses, and very little savings.

As the time came near to pay the travel agent, I was convinced that there was no way we would be able to go.

This was around the time when Promise Keepers, a popular movement in the 90s that called men to faith and integrity, was having their Million Man March in Washington DC. I really wanted to attend this event and I talked a buddy of mine into going with me. This smaller trip was easier to visualize as a reality, as the airfare to Washington was only about $300.

That evening, I announced to Susan that I was going to Washington.

"You can't," she retorted. "We're going to be in Thailand!"

"But we don't have the $10,000 to pay for our tickets."

"I believe we're going. I don't know how, but God is going to do it."

With that, I cancelled my reservation to go to Washington and my buddy ended up going without me.

Only a few days before our payment was due for the Thailand trip, we got a call from the travel agent saying that our tickets had been paid in full. Someone had come in and paid for our entire airfare anonymously!

The following year, we went to Thailand a second time, this time for nine months to oversee the orphanage, as the missionaries who ran the project had gone home on furlough.

As they were leaving, they informed us that the new property we had purchased needed the balance owing—about $35,000 USD—to be paid within two months, otherwise we would lose our down-payment and the property. I went into panic mode.

What kind of crazy deal is this? I thought. *Who signs such an agreement?*

But apparently this was common practice in Thailand.

At the time, Seeds of Hope was a very small organization. Our donors consisted of our friends, neighbors, and relatives. Not only did it seem impossible to raise $35,000, but I was embarrassed to mention that we would lose the down-payment we had made if we didn't come up with the money.

Susan's big idea was to fast and pray. On top of that, we should walk around the block every night praying out loud for the neighborhood.

I joined Susan and her friends in walking around the block praying the first evening, but I told her that it would be the last time. I felt foolish walking around praying out loud, being stared at by our Thai neighbors who were wondering what these crazy *farangs* (foreigners) were doing.

During this time, two things happened. The first is that I was getting ready to go to Cambodia to bring supplies to another orphanage.

AMAZING ABUNDANCE

The second is that Susan was driving to a local hospital when she got lost and found herself in the middle of a shanty slum. The houses were built on bamboo stilts and had thatched roofs. She saw children and women dressed in rags rummaging through garbage. The children were malnourished and half-naked, walking barefoot in garbage and filth.

She came home distressed about what she had just seen. Immediately she went into our storeroom and started pulling out duffle bags.

"What are you doing?" I asked.

After explaining what she had witnessed, she lamented that we had all these supplies that we weren't going to use. She planned to give them away to the poor.

"You can't do that," I warned her. "You're going to get mobbed."

The expression on her face told me she was passionate about this. "I'm going."

"But you'll be mobbed," I said again.

"I *am* going."

"Well, I'm not going with you."

After a conversation that lasted a few minutes, she drove off with a van loaded with duffle bags full of supplies.

I should add here that Susan is the strongest woman I know. She will do things that I don't think any other woman would do!

About two hours later, she returned, her hair a mess and her blouse pulled to one side.

"What happened?" I asked.

"I got mobbed."

"I told you that you were going to get mobbed. Why did you go?"

She then told the story of what had happened. When she'd arrived at the slum, women and children had started running out of their huts. The sliding door of the van was pulled open and people got in. Others climbed in through the back window, which had been left open because of the heat.

It was absolute mayhem, until the chief of the village was alerted to what was going on. He put a stop to everything. And after speaking to Susan, he asked her to come back on Sunday, at which time he would arrange the distribution of the goods.

It turned out that this chief was also a pastor. He invited us to his home at the church.

When Sunday morning came, this pastor had arranged everything. People were able to get supplies from us in an orderly fashion. There was a lot of gratitude and we felt humbled that these gifts meant so much to them. We, too, were overwhelmed with gratitude.

That day, we had an amazing time of worship at the pastor's house, which was constructed atop bamboo stilts, like all the other structures. The people of the church then asked me to speak about our mission and why I was travelling to Cambodia the next day. The small but fervent congregation prayed for me.

Afterward, they took up a small collection. People dropped their small coins in a straw-weaved basket.

As we were leaving, I asked the pastor, "Is this where you meet every Sunday?"

"Oh no," he said. "Normally we meet at our church."

He pointed to another bamboo building, this one without a roof, about a hundred yards away. He explained that the roof had caved in after a recent storm. That was the reason for the offering, he explained. They were raising money to buy iron sheets for a new roof.

"How much will it cost?" I asked.

In bhat, the Thai currency, it would be the equivalent of $250.

I made a quick decision. "Would it be okay if we donated to fix your roof?"

The next day, as I was on my way to the airport, we dropped off the money to pay for the church's new roof.

Upon my return from Cambodia a week later, Susan and I sat in the office of the orphanage. The deadline for the $35,000 payment was coming up in a week and we hadn't raised even a single dollar. I had a sick feeling in my stomach every time I thought about it.

AMAZING ABUNDANCE

We heard a knock at the door. It was one of the Thai caregivers, telling us that we had visitors.

We went out to meet two Japanese American couples from Hawaii. They were visiting ministries in the area, especially orphanages. They, too, had just returned from Cambodia, so we spoke of my recent trip, as well as what we were doing in Thailand.

Afterward we gave them a tour of the children's home and explained how we cared for the children. We showed them the nursey, the kitchen, the playroom, and the office.

As they were getting ready to leave, we stood in the foyer where we kept an architectural model of the new homes we were planning to build on the new property. One of the men was a pastor and was particularly interested in our building project. But I didn't want to talk about it because I knew that the property would be gone in a few days.

However, he kept asking about it.

"What are these buildings here?" he asked, pointing to the model.

I answered his question and tried to switch the subject, but he kept asking questions.

"When do you think you will start building?"

My heart sank. I didn't know how to reply.

"Well," I said, "we still have to make a big payment for the land before we can start building."

He seemed to make note of this, and then we resumed our pleasantries. They thanked us for the tour.

When they were leaving, this man took out his checkbook and wrote a check to the orphanage. He folded it in half and gave it to me. I promptly put it in my shirt pocket without thinking anything of it. After all, there was a donation box by the door and many visitors would leave money for the children's home as they left.

Susan and I went back into the office, returning to our thoughts of what we would do next. As we sat there, the thought came to me to look in my front pocket.

When I unfolded the check, I just about fell over in ecstasy. The check had been made out for $35,000! The praises rang out. "Hallelujah! Thank You, Jesus!"

Suddenly, a revelation came to me. I looked at Susan and asked, "Do you realize what just happened?"

"Yes," she replied with excitement in her voice. "Our prayers have been answered!"

"No. Don't you see? You were driving to the hospital when you got lost and ended up in the shanty. Those people were praying and saving their pennies to repair their church roof. For them, $250 was an astronomical amount, but for us it was nothing. You didn't know them and they didn't know us. You literally showed up out of the blue. Meanwhile, we were panicking because we needed $35,000, which to us was an astronomical amount. We were praying and pleading with God for what seemed like an impossible situation when these folks showed up from Hawaii. We didn't know them and they didn't know us. But it's obvious that God orchestrated the whole thing. For us, $35,000 was unobtainable. Not for this man! He simply wrote a check for the whole amount."

Since that time, I have seen this happen time and time again.

As you read this, let me encourage you to choose to believe in your dream despite any circumstance that suggest otherwise. By definition, miracles only happen in the midst of impossible situations. God is calling us to believe. Choose to believe, choose to love, choose to forgive, choose to have faith, and choose to live for God.

Chapter Thirteen

I ASKED GOD FOR A MILLION DOLLARS

Ask, and it will be given to you…
(Matthew 7:7)

IS IT REALLY that simple? Ask and you shall receive? Yes! God is a good Father and He loves to give good gifts to His children. As a good Father, He also discerns what is best for us.

When my son was about seven years old, I asked him what he wanted for Christmas. Our friends are hunters and he had seen their rifles and was quite fascinated with firearms. He told me that he wanted a high-powered rifle with a scope.

That Christmas, he received a skateboard. I knew that he couldn't handle a rifle. He had nowhere to shoot it or store it, not to mention all the safety concerns. Even though I could have easily bought him a rifle, it would have been inappropriate.

However, when he was fourteen years old I bought him a .22-calibre rifle and enrolled both of us in a firearms safety program. Since that time, we have both enjoyed hunting and shooting together.

In the same way, God knows when it's appropriate to give us our prayer requests. God always answers prayer. It's either yes, no, or wait. Knowing that God is a good Father, and trusting that He knows best, we can rest in His sovereign will.

As the ministry grew, we wanted to serve where the need was greatest. Through prayer and a series of events, we ended up in

Zambia, the epicenter of the HIV/AIDS epidemic. We started there in 2000, and by 2005 we'd bought an additional seventy-two acres to develop into a boarding school for HIV-infected or -affected orphaned children.

We started building in 2006. According to the plans, Grace Academy would have eight children's homes, an office, a clinic, a cafeteria, staff housing, a recreation hall, and a school covering Grades One to Twelve. We funded the building project through fundraisers and applying for grants.

As I considered how large our vision had become, I felt overwhelmed. At one point I remember asking God for a million dollars. I recall that conversation with God, explaining what I would do with the money, how we would be able to provide loving homes, medical care, nutrition, and education to children who had been abandoned and cast away because of HIV and the fear and stigma associated with it. These children were grieving the loss of their parents and had been rejected by their extended family. Not to mention the malnutrition and disease!

Despite explaining all this from my heart, nothing seemed to change.

We just kept on building. We finished one building and moved on to the next. Money seemed to come in as we needed it.

After a year, I looked back and realized that more than a million dollars had come in! And since that time, more than ten million dollars has been poured into Grace Academy. We now have eighteen children's homes on site, along with staff housing, a preschool, an elementary school, and a high school. We produce our own electricity with solar panels and grow most of our own food. We have our own church and are becoming more and more self-sustaining.

God has been so faithful in supplying all our needs. He has far surpassed anything we could have ever imagined. When we look back at all the accomplishments, we are in awe.

What about in our personal lives? Does God care about our wealth? Can we ask Him to prosper us? I would emphatically say yes!

In Jeremiah 29:11, the Lord declares, *"For I know the plans I have for you... plans to prosper you and not to harm you, plans to give you hope and a future."*

As I was planning to write this book, I asked God for a specific amount in my bank account and in a certain amount of time. Now, I don't ever remember Jesus praying that way, giving God a schedule. However, remember that people with goals achieve them. I was willing to do my part, and all that it would take to realize that goal was to believe in God to do His part. It is important to me that what I write is also true in my life. I do have amazing abundance. In fact, as I count my blessings, I realize that I've been blessed beyond measure.

Here is one of my favorite scriptures:

Which of you, if your son asks for bread, will give him a stone? Or if he asks for a fish, will give him a snake? If you, then, though you are evil, know how to give good gifts to your children, how much more will your Father in heaven give good gifts to those who ask him! (Matthew 7:9–11)

When Susan and I met, we had both come out of bad relationships. We were broken people. Our dream was simply to raise a family. We just wanted to buy a home and raise our kids. We didn't aspire to do great things. Nothing in our education or finances indicated that we would do anything more than that.

It all started for us in 1995 when Susan heard about the plight of AIDS orphans in Thailand and wanted to help. We started with a group of friends, collecting pop bottles and baking pies to raise money. We had no idea how much this ministry would grow.

As the ministry expanded, we kept seeing God answer prayers in the most amazing ways.

What I have written here is what I have learned in our faith walk, in our personal finances, in our relationships, in our health, and in every other area in our lives. We changed our mindsets to believe and kept asking our Father to bless us.

I want to encourage you to follow these principles. They are not mine; they are based on God's word.

Chapter Fourteen

THE BLESSING OF GENEROSITY

*He has sent me to proclaim freedom
for the prisoners...*
(Luke 4:18)

MONEY IS A spiritual matter, and what you do with it has eternal value. Wealth will magnify your character. If you were generous before you were wealthy, you will be even more so afterward—and if you were stingy before wealth, you will become even stingier. If you were kind when you were poor, you will find even more ways to be kind once you have more money, whereas if you used people before, you will only grow more insecure and abusive. Wealth will reflect your true character.

Here's something to remember: God is more interested in your character than your wealth.

Part of understanding wealth is that everything we have has been entrusted to us. We are merely stewards and don't take anything with us when we go.

To me, the real blessing is what we do with what God has entrusted to us. God said to Abraham, "I will bless you and make you a blessing" (Genesis 12:1, paraphrased). Isn't that a wonderful promise?

Not everyone can be a missionary and travel to far-off lands. But we are all called to do *something*. There are those who go. And just as importantly, there are those who send resources, pray, and make these ministries possible.

A huge part of the blessing of wealth is giving—and here is the paradox: the more you give, the more you have.

> *Give, and it will be given to you. A good measure, pressed down, shaken together and running over, will be poured into your lap. For with the measure you use, it will be measured to you.* (Luke 6:38)

And about the tithe, the Bible writes:

> *"Bring the whole tithe into the storehouse, that there may be food in my house. Test me in this," says the Lord Almighty, "and see if I will not throw open the floodgates of heaven and pour out so much blessing that there will not be room enough to store it."* (Malachi 3:10)

The tithe is a controversial topic for many people. Some say it's a bygone commandment as we no longer live under the law but under grace. Others say they can't afford to tithe.

But remember that God doesn't need your money. He spoke the universe and everything in it into being. In the same way, He can turn the sand of the deserts into diamonds and the rocks of the fields into gold. So He needs nothing from us.

I look at the tithe as an opportunity to share in the Kingdom of God. It is a blessing!

Let me ask you something. Imagine that God said to you, "For every dollar I give you, give me back ten cents. I will bless the work of your hands, keep calamity and mishaps from you, protect what is yours, and multiply your wealth." Would you do it?

Well, this is exactly what He is saying.

To me, the tithe is an act of worship, faith, and obedience. The truth of its promise has been shown to me over and over. To those who say they can't afford to tithe, I say that you can't afford not to. People always seem to have money for what's important to them, and then they might give what's left over to God.

When you tithe, it means putting God first.

Tithing will set your spending aright, because it puts God first. When that happens, you will find that you don't spend on frivolous things or go into debt. That's the first blessing. The second blessing is supernatural. God will meet your needs and provide riches without adding any trouble to it. Jesus said it best: *"But seek first his kingdom and his righteousness, and all these things will be given to you as well"* (Matthew 6:33).

At the beginning of the book, I made a strong statement: you are where you are because you choose to be there. There are, however, people who cannot escape the harsh reality they're in; these people are children who are born into extreme poverty and abuse. They are vulnerable and defenseless. They can't fend for themselves.

God is concerned for the vulnerable. James 1:27 reads, *"Religion that God our Father accepts as pure and faultless is this: to look after orphans and widows in their distress and to keep oneself from being polluted by the world."*

Seeds of Hope cares for orphaned and vulnerable children. We started caring for HIV-orphaned children who were abandoned and left to die. We now care for other vulnerable children, including those who have experienced war and the murder of their parents. Our newest project is building a home for children under the age of ten who have been rescued from human trafficking in Thailand. An unspeakable evil!

Child sponsorship enables us to provide loving homes, nurture, medical care, emotional healing, education, and hope. These children have come to us traumatized and bewildered by the loss of their parents, abandoned by their extended family, and affected by disease, homelessness, and hunger. At our ministry, they find love, acceptance, and security. We are able to share the love of Christ and convey that God loves them. We show them that they are special and precious, and that God has a plan for their lives. Despite what they've gone through, God has not abandoned them.

Our child sponsorship program costs a little over one dollar per day and changes the life and destiny of a child. As you consider your financial growth, would you consider sponsoring a child?[5]

---

[5] To learn more, please visit our website: www.seedsofhopecm.com.

Conclusion

MY PRAYER, AS you come to the end of this book, is that you have made a commitment to start believing in better things for yourself and your family, that you will make the financial decisions that will make your hard-earned money grow, and that you will experience the wealth that the Lord has for you. It's a journey and takes time, but remember that good financial decisions plus time equals exponential growth.

Above all, I pray that you experience God doing the miraculous for you.

We all desire well-being, prosperity, and growth. However, none of this happens by chance and from the safety of your comfort zone. If you want different results in your finances, you'll have to change the way you live—and in particular, you'll have to change your mindset.

You'll also have to evaluate your subconscious limitations and remove them. Start believing in better things for yourself. Watch your thoughts. Pay attention to your self-talk and remove the phrase "I can't" from your vocabulary; the moment you say "I can't," you've already made a decision.

Learn to catch your negative thoughts and transform them into positive thoughts. And change the way you speak. After all, your words are a reflection of what you really think and what is in your heart.

John F. Kennedy, upon granting Winston Churchill honorary American citizenship on April 9, 1963, said, "He mobilized the English language and sent it into battle."[6] What a powerful saying! This makes

---

[6] "Quotes FAQ," *International Churchill Society*. Date of access: July 13, 2022 (https://winstonchurchill.org/resources/quotes/quotes-faq/).

me think of Proverbs 18:21, which tells us, *"The tongue has the power of life and death..."*

What if we rallied our words and sent them off to war? What if we chose the way we talked to ourselves and spoke life and empowerment to ourselves instead of negativity? What if we intentionally spoke words of love and encouragement to those we love? What if we continually lifted up those around us by the words we spoke to them? What would our lives look like?

Here's a thought: whatever you're going through, you are stronger than you think, smarter than you think, braver than you think, can endure more than you think, can do more than you think, and can give more than you think. We are blessed beyond measure.

Yet we take these blessings for granted and aren't careful in our thoughts, actions, and the way in which we spend money and live our lives. I would like to encourage you to be more intentional in all areas of your life.

As I write this, we're still in the middle of the COVID-19 crisis. We've seen lockdowns that have caused economic turmoil in addition to human suffering. There is a lot of instability in the financial world as governments go deeper in debt and print more money. Inflation keeps going higher, devaluing our dollar. Now more than ever, people need to be careful and wise in their financial dealings and prepare for the economic hardships ahead. Proverbs 22:3 states, *"The prudent see danger and take refuge, but the simple keep going and pay the penalty."*

I want to be careful not to instill fear. What I want to convey is that we can be prepared and prosperous even in difficult times. I can't tell you what to do, where to put your money, or where to invest, because we're all different and our financial situations vary. However, I believe it is prudent that we have a plan for our families. We should have an emergency fund, then get out of debt with cash on hand. We should invest our money where it can grow and be protected against inflation.

Above all, though, we must place our hope in God.

In Chapter One, we looked at a table which showed the difference wealth makes in the lives of people around the world. On one side, we read of the benefits to being wealthy; the other side showed us the hardships of being poor.

Life is hard. Being poor is hard. Getting wealthy is hard.

However, one hard way leads to a dead-end whereas the other hard way leads to financial independence. You get to choose your hard path.

Here's to your amazing abundance!

About the Author

JOHN CHALKIAS SERVES as the executive director and co-founder of Seeds of Hope Children's Ministry, an organization that helps orphaned children, primarily those affected or infected by HIV/AIDS. The ministry provides housing, medical care, and education for the children in their care.

John and this ministry love innovation, creativity, and thinking outside the box, which has led the ministry to also serve children affected by disease, war, and human trafficking in some of the poorest countries in the world. His desire is to help people, no matter what their circumstance or where they live, to move out of poverty into abundant and victorious living. John is an ordained minister, missionary, public speaker, and writer. This book is a follow up to his book, *You Too Can Have An Amazing Life*.

Drawing on his rich experience overseas, in this book he maps out a plan to help people experience amazing abundance.

John and his wife Susan live in Chilliwack, British Columbia, Canada.

www.facebook.com/amazinglife4you/
www.johnchalkias.ca